SERGEI O. PROKOFIEFF, born in Moscow in 1954, studied fine arts and painting at the Moscow School of Art. He encountered anthroposophy in his youth, and soon made the decision to devote his life to it. He has been active as an author and lecturer since 1982, and in 1991 he co-founded the Anthroposophical Society in Russia. In Easter 2001 he became a member of the Executive Council of the General Anthroposophical Society in Dornach. He is the author of many books available in many languages throughout the world.

DATE DUE

APR 0 4 2013		
SEP 1 2 2013		
NOV 2 8 2014		
GAYLORD		PRINTED IN U.S.A.

D1247749

By the same author:

Why Become a Member of the School of Spiritual Science?

SERGEI O. PROKOFIEFF

TEMPLE LODGE

Translated from German by Maria St. Goar

Temple Lodge Publishing
Hillside House, The Square
Forest Row, RH18 5ES

www.templelodge.com

Published by Temple Lodge 2012

Originally published in German under the title *Warum wird man Mitglied der Freien Hochschule für Geisteswissenschaft?* by Verlag am Goetheanum, Dornach, 2010 (edited by Ute E. Fischer)

A catalogue record for this book is available from the British Library

ISBN 978 1 906999 39 1

Cover layout based on original design by Sven Baumann, incorporating the logo of the School of Spiritual Science, Switzerland
Typeset by DP Photosetting, Neath, West Glamorgan
Printed and bound by Gutenberg Press, Malta

Contents

Preface

The content of this booklet corresponds to a large extent with the first chapter of my book *Die Erste Klasse der Michael-Schule und ihre christologischen Grundlagen* (The First Class of the Michael School and Its Christological Foundations) published in German in 2009. The numerous lectures that I gave for many years at various weekend conferences about the First Class, which then became the basis of the above-named book, were addressed by virtue of their contents only to members of the School of Spiritual Science. Consequently, the book that originated from these lectures was likewise directed only to this circle of individuals.

It was a completely different matter in the case of the lecture that represents the basis of this text. On every occasion, it preceded the First Class conference and was thus addressed to a much larger circle, namely to all members of the Anthroposophical Society. Again and again, it turned out that for some people this lecture became the occasion to call to mind the question of membership in the First Class in a much more conscious form, and following that to take the decisive step of entering the Michael School.

This experience gave rise to the occasion for printing this lecture separately for interested individuals, as a stimulus to consider their relationship to the Michael School on Earth against the background of the karma that guides human beings in their present incarnation to anthroposophy.

In this sense, the present text may well be an aid for some interested individuals to grasp to its full extent the unique significance of the establishment of the Esoteric School — carried out as it was by Rudolf Steiner based on the Michael Spirit — so as to gain the courage and will to become a member in it out of full inner conviction. For the fact that, as disciples of Michael from their prenatal sojourns, all anthroposophists bear in themselves the connection to the supersensible School of Michael and its imaginative cultus — and if this fact actually enters their awareness — then this must turn into the earnest longing to join, together with other human beings, to assume the corresponding part of responsibility for this Michael institution on Earth.

Thus this booklet is addressed above all to those human beings on the path of Michaelic discipleship who struggle with the question of their relationship to him. This can then become the incentive to respond to this question by becoming a member of the Michael School.

Sergei O. Prokofieff
Goetheanum, Easter 2010

Why Become a Member of the First Class of the Michael School?

Abstract ideals will be replaced by concrete ideals corresponding to forward moving evolution. If that does not succeed, the Earth would submerge into materialism and humanity would have to start over again — following a great catastrophe — either on Earth itself or on a near planet. The Earth needs anthroposophy! One who understands that is an anthroposophist.
— Rudolf Steiner, lecture of 27 February 1910[1]

If one surveys the development of anthroposophy in the course of the twentieth century, one finds that several thoughts, like red threads, run through this development. When one tries to grasp these thoughts and examines them more closely, one can arrive at a deeper understanding of anthroposophy's nature. As such, a thought that links the beginning of anthroposophy with its conclusion — to the extent that its unfolding could still be carried out by Rudolf Steiner himself — can be seen in a fact he expressed, namely that anthroposophy did not originate from human arbitrariness nor out of a necessity of humanity, but as an answer to a mighty *call* from the spiritual world.

Now, when considering the, at that time, 25-year-long history of anthroposophy on Earth in this light, one can discover three calls out of the spiritual world as their foundation. Rudolf Steiner mentions the first of these calls already in early lectures inasmuch as he compares the present-day situation of humanity with the concluding age on ancient Atlantis. Just as a small group of people had to be prepared at the end of the Atlantean epoch in order to begin the great post-Atlantean age, so the present time has matured to the point where people are found among humankind who gradually form a nucleus for the next greater epoch that will begin after the seventh (final) post-Atlantean cultural period. So, just as a spiritual call went out to certain people that had been chosen for a future task at the end of the Atlantean time, so it is the case in our time.

In the lectures from the year 1909, Rudolf Steiner points in this regard particularly to the fact that out of the circle of masters of esoteric Christendom, who he also designated as the 'Masters of Wisdom and Harmony of Feeling', a call had gone out to human beings. It was a call that initially led to the establishment of the Theosophical Society. For according to the words of Rudolf Steiner, its founding in 1875 in New York first had a distinctly Western, that is Rosicrucian, character. (See GA 216, 'Barr Manuscript', Part III.)[2]

This first attempt had not been successful, however. And after the Theosophical Society had ultimately diverted from its original direction, having through the one-sided oriental influences increasingly become a puppet of various occult interests, Rudolf Steiner, by taking charge of the German Section, made the tremendous attempt to lead the Society back to its roots. He recalls: 'This was the situation. I found myself facing the necessity to join the Theosophical Society. Genuine initiates had stood by at its inauguration, and due to that, even though ensuing events had exhibited certain imperfections, it is *for now* an instrument for the spiritual life of the present' (ibid., emphasis by Rudolf Steiner).

Now, this first call differed fundamentally from the one in the Atlantean age. Then, it was only a matter of a number of human beings who were chosen by the initiates of the great Sun Oracle and their mighty leader whom Rudolf Steiner called a Christ-initiate (GA 13). Those human beings were chosen for the task of preparing and initiating the great post-Atlantean epoch. Now, however, the call went out *to all human beings*. This is why those who voluntarily receive anthroposophy into themselves today can reply to this spiritual call by following the inner path that it opens up to us. Rudolf Steiner expressed it like this: 'At that time [in Atlantis], it was the great initiate [Manu] who in a similar manner gathered human beings around himself; today it is the Masters of Wisdom and Harmony of Feelings; their call goes out to all of you' (GA 109/111, 6 April 1909). And in another lecture: 'At that time in ancient Atlantis, it was important to find the connection with the physical, the sensory world. Today, the task is to rediscover the spiritual, the spirit world. Even as in those days the ancient initiate gathered his group together *locally* — as his call went out to the scorned humble ones — so once again today under different conditions [*not locally* but to all human beings], a call goes out by the great Masters of Wisdom who allow a certain spiritual measure of wisdom to flow into humankind' (GA 109/111, 10 June 1909).

A little later, Rudolf Steiner speaks of a second call. This one did not go out anymore from several masters of esoteric Christianity, but from *one* of them who bears the name *Christian Rosenkreutz*. This occurred in December 1911, when Rudolf Steiner undertook the founding of a small esoteric group within the German Section of the Theosophical Society that was led by him. It was to be called 'The Endowment for Theosophical Way of Life and Art' [*Stiftung für theosophische Art und Kunst*] and initially included only twelve people whom Rudolf Steiner had gathered in preparation for a special esoteric mission. It was intended, however, gradually to release this group from Rudolf Steiner's leadership and later on to place it under the direct guidance of Christian Rosenkreutz.

In regard to this endowment that could not be continued for certain reasons, the description of which would go beyond the framework of these considerations, Rudolf Steiner told Marie Steiner in a conversation that it is always a matter of three calls that resound *for a certain age* from the spiritual world. If they would not be heard by human beings, then mankind would have to wait for a very long time until such a favourable opportunity would once again come to pass for them.

In the year 1912, Rudolf Steiner now speaks of this second founding — especially after it had been unsuccessful — in such a way that with it the second call had also died away and one would then have to wait and see whether a third call might still ensue, and see if human beings might still hearken to it as a last opportunity. Furthermore, if this third call would be to no avail as had already been stated, one would have to wait a very long time until the spiritual world would once more have such confidence in humanity — to put it in human words — that yet again three calls would resound. Marie Steiner noted his words down at that time as follows: 'It was as if

6

it were a direct communication from the spiritual world. It was like a call brought close to humanity — then the spiritual world would await the kind of echo that comes to meet this call. As a rule, such a call should occur three times. If the call would fade away without being heard even the third time, it would be withdrawn again into the spiritual world for long ages. One time this call had already been brought towards humanity; unfortunately it found no echo. This is the second time. One deals here with purely spiritual matters. Each unsuccessful occasion causes conditions and correlations to become more diffi-cult' (GA 264, 15 December 1911).

If we read this conversation today, which has been published in the intervening time, the weighty question arises immediately: Where in the development of the anthroposophical movement do we find the third call? The movement's history demonstrates clearly that it had resounded through this movement at the Christmas Conference.

Now, before we go into more detail in regard to this third call, it must be pointed out briefly that, already during the opening lecture of the Christmas Conference, the motif of the spiritual call appeared in a quite special way. On 24 December 1924, Rudolf Steiner says: 'Now today more than ever before we may call to mind that a spiritual movement such as the one we have embraced with the name "anthroposophical" is not born out of any earthly arbitrary consideration. At the very beginning of our conference, I therefore want to start by reminding you that it was in the last third of the nineteenth century that on the one hand the waves of materialism were rising high, while on the other a remarkable revelation struck down into these waves from the other side of the world; a revelation from something spiritual that can be received from powers of spiritual life by those individuals whose mind and soul are in a receptive state. A revelation of the spirit was opened up for humankind, and not from any arbitrary earthly consideration, *but in obedience to a call resounding from the spiritual world*; not from any arbitrary earthly consideration, but through a vision of the sublime pictures given out of the spiritual world as modern revelations for the spiritual life of mankind. From this flowed the impulse for the anthroposophical movement. This anthroposophical movement is not an act of service to the Earth; in its totality and all its details this anthroposophical movement is a service to the gods, a service to God. We create the right mood for it when we see it in all its totality as such a service to God' (GA 260).

For all those who heard these words then, and likewise for anthroposophists who read them today, it was and is absolutely clear that Rudolf Steiner speaks here about the new revelations by Michael as the present Time Spirit and spiritual leader of humanity. The references to the 'last third of the nineteenth century' and 'the sublime pictures' as the spiritual origin of the anthroposophical movement — images that are linked with Michael's supersensible cultus concerning which Rudolf Steiner speaks later on in the karma lectures — are evidence of this. Likewise, the characterization of anthroposophy as a 'divine service, a service to God', point out that it is not a *call* here by several great initiates or only by one, but a call that resounded from the hierarchical beings themselves and — before all others — from the Time Spirit Michael, who leads them all.[3]

8

That this call actually went out from Michael himself was also confirmed by Rudolf Steiner's words in the sixth evening lecture during the Christmas Conference. 'Only at the end of the nineteenth century, beginning from the seventies, a *new call*, so to speak, approached from the spiritual heights towards humanity. The age began which I have often characterized as the Michael age' (GA 233, 29 December 1923).

Now, Rudolf Steiner once characterized the genuine Masters of esoteric Christendom as having a direct relationship to the hierarchies: 'These Masters of Wisdom who stand in a direct relationship with the forces of the higher hierarchies...' (GA 159/160, 15 June 1915). For the context of our considerations, this means that they are the mediators between these hierarchical powers of the spiritual world and earthly mankind. This is why they could also pass on the mighty spiritual call that had resounded in the last third of the nineteenth century from the Michael Sphere to human beings. And thus was the transmission of this Michael-call indeed carried out. First this ensued throughout the entirety of the Rosicrucian Masters during the *original* establishment of the Theosophical Society; then through *one* leading initiate of eso-

Great Michael Call		
1st Call: 1875 through the Masters of Wisdom and Harmony of Feelings[5]	2nd Call: 1911 through Christian Rosenkreutz	3rd Call: 1923 through Rudolf Steiner

teric Christendom, Christian Rosenkreutz. Ultimately, as a last attempt, it was brought about through Rudolf Steiner as the new Master of Wisdom and Harmony of Feelings[4] during the Christmas Conference.

The thus documented connection of the Rosicrucian Masters with the Michael impulse of the present will not surprise us.[6] For Rudolf Steiner points out more than once that most of all the genuine Rosicrucians always sought a relationship to Michael in the spiritual world. Earlier, however, prior to his present period of leadership among mankind, which has begun in 1879, they could only find him in a sort of dream-state. 'Rosicrucianism is denoted by the fact that its most enlightened minds had a powerful longing to encounter Michael, but could do so only as if in a dream. Since the end of the last third of the nineteenth century, human beings can encounter Michael in a conscious manner' (GA 233a, 13 January 1924).[7] As was likewise described in detail elsewhere, at the end of the nineteenth century Rudolf Steiner was the *first Rosicrucian* who with full consciousness encountered Michael in the directly adjacent spiritual world.[8]

While in this sense the above-characterized mighty call by Michael is deeply connected with the three other calls and forms their spiritual background as one is wont to say, this call can, however, not be directly added to them. This call could be heard in the last third of the nineteenth century only by initiates and their pupils (in contrast to the other three calls that were directed also at people who were not initiated). For the hearing of this mighty call was linked with the clairvoyant perception of the new imaginative Michael revelations; revelations that Rudolf Steiner could behold in the spiritual world adjacent to the Earth.

And as an answer to this call he decided at the beginning of the twentieth century to establish anthroposophy on Earth.

Only much later, after the founding of the *New Mysteries* at the Christmas Conference,[9] this mighty call became altogether accessible to all human beings through Rudolf Steiner's mediation.

If today one diligently studies the shorthand reports of the Christmas Conference, one can ascertain that the whole Conference was pervaded, as it were, by a powerful call. As early as during the Foundation Stone laying on 25 December 1923, this powerful call becomes apparent through the threefold call, 'Soul of Man!' at the beginning of the three segments of the Foundation Stone verse, and at its ending through a further threefold call, 'May Human Beings Hear It!' It was reported to me, by individuals who were present at the Christmas Conference, how Rudolf Steiner himself had intoned such 'called-out' words.[10] From him they actually sounded like a mighty call. And all those who heard him immediately had the impression that here it was not a matter of a personal call by Rudolf Steiner, but that he himself was the conscious mediator of the third call out of the spiritual world. This is why it also said in the programme of the Christmas Conference: 'Foundation Stone Laying of the International Anthroposophical Society *through* Rudolf Steiner' (GA 260).

There is a passage in the documentations of the Christmas Conference that can easily be overlooked because, in the short and most familiar excerpt from them, which contains the texts of the Foundation Stone laying and the rhythms, this segment was omitted. We deal here with the somewhat longer introduction by Rudolf Steiner preceding the first rhythm of the Foundation Stone verse on 26 December. There, he speaks of the contemporary relationship of human beings to the spiritual world, and of the fact that in this context something definitive is happening in our time that people could and also must become aware of. Rudolf Steiner formulates this description so that it is not difficult to distinguish three stages in it that follow one upon the other.

First he says that, through what is now coming out of the spiritual world towards the human being during the Christmas Conference, one must feel an intensified responsibility towards everything one does out of spirit knowledge and would still wish to do in the future. The second — and in this connection probably the most important matter — is that something has actually happened in the spiritual world that emerges from there like a new spiritual impulse. And human beings of the present are challenged to follow this impulse out of their own free will. At the end of this introduction, Rudolf Steiner states very briefly that human beings today must allow themselves to be permeated by this new spirit impulse. Thus, three successive steps are here to be gone through. First we have the acceptance of inner responsibility regarding the new spiritual impulse, then the possibility to follow this impulse, and finally, on the third stage, to allow oneself to be permeated by it.

At this point the words in which Rudolf Steiner describes the *second* stage will be quoted, because they are of decisive significance for the entire esoteric event of the Christmas Conference. The way in which the words are formulated makes it unambiguously clear that Rudolf Steiner relates all three stages of what actually happened in the spiritual world during the Christmas Conference. He says: 'The spiritual world wants to achieve something with humanity *at this particular moment in historical evolution*. It wants to achieve this in the most varied realms of life, and it is up to us clearly and truly to follow the impulses from the spiritual world' (GA 260, 26 December 1923).

Linking up with this theme again, Rudolf Steiner says — and with this the first rhythm is already introduced — that he would like to repeat the words of the Foundation Stone verse once more; words 'that by the will of the spiritual world were spoken to you yesterday' (ibid.). Saying this does not only indicate that the words of the Foundation Stone verse originate directly out of the spiritual world, but that they contain *a call out of that world* with which they start the verse three times: 'Soul of Man' or 'Human Soul'. If one also takes the preceding words by Rudolf Steiner into consideration, that the spiritual world has something quite real in mind at the present moment in regard to human beings, from this situation it becomes understandable that 'at the present moment' indeed refers to the Christmas Conference.

Two decisive questions arise from this: From *whom* does this third call actually sound forth? And can one find an answer based on the content of the Christmas Conference on one's own?

Now, it might be assumed that an answer to this question had already been given. Conveyed through Rudolf Steiner, the call comes from Michael himself, whose name, perhaps for this reason, is given only one time during the Christmas Conference in connection with the word 'call'.[11] Yet the fact alone that, except for this one

13

occasion, Michael is not mentioned by name throughout the entire Christmas Conference — not even in its esoteric segments — says something and signifies, as we shall still see, that another spiritual being was involved in the mediation of this call; something that in the following will be dealt with in more detail. For that being occupied a key position in a certain regard for the esoteric comprehension of the entire Christmas Conference.

Besides, from the above-quoted passage of the opening address, it becomes unmistakably clear that the mighty call by Michael, which had resounded in the last third of the nineteenth century (that had begun in the year 1867 as already mentioned) and the hearing of which had led to the establishment of the anthroposophical movement at the beginning of the twentieth century through Rudolf Steiner, is not identical with the *first* of the three calls referred to in 1911. Rudolf Steiner did say at the time of the second call (1911) that the first one had already unsuccessfully faded away. Yet concerning the anthroposophical movement, this could in no way be alleged considering the way it was presented in the opening address, since this movement had been successfully established by Rudolf Steiner almost ten years earlier, and since then had unfolded in ever increasing form. If that had not been the case, he could not have referred to it in the way he then did during the opening of the Christmas Conference.

*

Before we go into more detail concerning the secret of the entity that is deeply connected with Michael, and whose call penetrates the entire Christmas Conference as if on

14

behalf of Michael, it is necessary to look briefly into the three most important consequences of the Christmas Conference itself. Rudolf Steiner emphatically points out that the Christmas Conference, which in a purely outward manner had been brought to a close on 1 January 1924, should — so he added — never end, as far as its inner esoteric aspect within the Anthroposophical Society is concerned. 'While we did formally close, in actual fact this Christmas Conference should never be closed but continue on in the life of the Anthroposophical Society' (GA 260a, 6 February 1924). This is '...because the Christmas Conference only becomes real through what it will become further on' (ibid.). Thus, Rudolf Steiner himself kept on living this Christmas Conference impulse, whereby three main consequences eventually emerged from it:

- The first consequence was the great karma revelations that were presented in a cycle of 82 lectures.
- The second consisted in the establishment of the School of Spiritual Science with its heart — the First Class — that he designated as the Michael School on Earth.
- And third was the creation of the model for the subsequently erected second Goetheanum.

Let us look at the karma lectures to begin with. In doing so, one soon becomes aware that the communications about the karma of the Anthroposophical Society represent their culmination. Actually, these research-results dealt with the karma of the *anthroposophical movement*, in the womb of which future anthroposophy was still being prepared in the spiritual world under the direct guidance of Michael. Rudolf Steiner, however, consistently used a different formulation. Repeatedly, he said at corresponding passages that he would now speak about the karma of the *Anthroposophical Society*, meaning the karma of a very real community of human beings who here on Earth have made the conscious decision to become its members. With this, the Anthroposophical Society finds itself in a quite special situation within contemporary humanity. To this day, it is probably the only human community on Earth that actually knows its own karma; in any case, in a form and scope that are completely unique. While presently large numbers of spiritual, religious, occult movements and groupings exist in this world, only the Anthroposophical Society possesses such karma-knowledge as a basis for people's living and working together.

We moreover find out from these lectures that, before it could appear on Earth, anthroposophy passed through two developmental stages in the spiritual world. The first was Michael's supersensible School from the fifteenth to the eighteenth century, where many human souls shared in the spiritual instruction by Michael in the lofty Sun-Spheres. Since these souls had passed through this School, during their next incarnation on Earth they felt the powerful impulse to seek for anthroposophy in its earthly form, and to absorb it intensely into their very being.

Rudolf Steiner designates as the second stage of the supersensible preparation of anthroposophy the imaginative cultus from the end of the eighteenth to the beginning of the nineteenth century in the spiritual world adjacent to the Earth. In this cultus, the contents of the Michael School were taken up once again, but now in a more imaginative–cultic form so that the human beings who participated in it — and these were for the largest part those souls who had been present already in the supersensible Michael School — could receive these contents all the way into the will-foundations of their being. Due to this, subsequently on Earth they carried within themselves the initiative-filled impulse to be active and creative based on anthroposophy. 'Become a human being with initiative' (GA 237, 4 August 1924); everyone carries this impulse in his or her karma who has once participated in the Michael Cultus.[12]

For these human souls, a further consequence of such supersensible experiences was that, through their encounter with anthroposophy on Earth, they could remember having participated in both stages of anthroposophy's preparation and as a result discovered something like a promise or pledge within themselves to want to become servants or helpers of Michael on Earth. In other words now, out of a deepest heart's desire, they sought to fulfil what Michael had entrusted them with, both in his Sun-School and during the supersensible cultus. For everything that takes place in this way in the spiritual world is under no circumstances only a transmission of wisdom. At the same time it is also a task (or mission) implanted into the karma of the individual in question. Such a task concerns his or her innermost essence of heart and mind, and for this reason can become the very meaning of such a person's earthly life.

These two stages of anthroposophy's supersensible preparation are the ones best known among anthroposophists. Less familiar is a single reference by Rudolf Steiner, that in the spiritual world these two stages were preceded by a third one. In the time-sequence, this third stage is actually the first one, for it occurred in the spiritual world at the beginning of the Michael School and accompanied its very first unfolding. Rudolf Steiner speaks about this only once in the karma lecture of 28 July 1924 (GA 237), where he describes this 'mighty event' as the 'cosmic tempest'. It is about the fact that during the time when the Michael School began its activity in the Sun Sphere under the leadership of Michael, a mighty cosmic event was to have occurred in the spiritual world. It was one of those events that happen only very rarely in world evolution. The last time this was the case, Rudolf Steiner goes on to say, was in the Atlantean age. Only in the course of such great intervals do events of this sort take place in the spiritual world in which, not only the Third and Second Hierarchy, but most of all the highest First Hierarchy is involved. At that time, through the activity of those beings at the beginning of the epoch of the con-sciousness soul (1413), human nature was thoroughly transformed from out of the heights of the spiritual world — even though, as Rudolf Steiner emphasizes, earthly human beings themselves perceived almost nothing of this outwardly.[13] Yet, this event was cognized and experienced that much more intensely by those souls who were gathered around Michael in his supersensible School at the end of the fourteenth and beginning of the fifteenth century.

Rudolf Steiner describes this event itself by saying that at this time the First Hierarchy — which alone possesses the ability to imprint the spiritual into the earthly — guided a spiritual substance (that, according to its nature, was cosmic thought-substance) out of the domain of the Second Hierarchy — which as we know is especially united with the Sun — over onto the Earth, and imprinted it into the human being out of the cosmos as new substance of intelligence. With this, human beings were transformed at this time so that, having formerly been heart-beings, they now became beings of the head. Yet we must not connect this with what in ordinary life we understand to be heart and head. Here we deal with far more essential processes.

For those human souls who were gathered around Michael at that time, this transformation of the earthly human being appeared as follows. The whole of Earth was enveloped, as it were, by a raging, inundating mighty tempest accompanied by spiritual thunderbolts and lightning flashes. Even though terrestrial human beings could not perceive it, this spiritual thunderstorm had a profound effect upon the whole of human culture. For we know that precisely around this time (the end of the fourteenth and beginning of the fifteenth century) the so-called modern age commenced on Earth.

Despite the direct influence of this cosmic happening upon all earthly configurations, this was a process that encompasses much larger spans of time than it takes for the development of just one soul member in humanity (in this case the consciousness soul). The short reference by Rudolf Steiner, that a comparable event occurred last on ancient Atlantis, allows us to have a faint inkling of what this more recent happening might have consisted. During the Atlantean age, human nature was re-shaped in such a way that cosmic intelligence — which man carried earlier only in the limb-system — was lifted up by the hierarchies from this realm into the region of the heart. Provided that this assumption is correct, one could trace this process back still further and imagine that in the ancient Lemurian age the cosmic intelligence was guided for *the very first time* through the activity of the First Hierarchy (in unison with the Sun forces of the Second Hierarchy), and just into the limb system of the human being.

This process would also have been of special significance because — as we know from other descriptions by Rudolf Steiner — it was in the Lemurian age that the human being received the 'I' and with that his/her human evolution generally began as an individual ego-being. This is why the two events on ancient Lemuria must be viewed concurrently; namely the 'I'-bestowing on man through the Spirits of Form on the one hand, and on the other (as the basis for this) the simultaneous receiving of the cosmic intelligence into the human limb system through the deeds of the First Hierarchy. On this basis, one can comprehend the entire inner development of humanity on Earth. For as long as the cosmic intelligence (and with that the individual ego) was only effective in the system of the limbs, the human being was still completely dependent on the spiritual world, the world of the hierarchies. Then, during the Atlantean age, when this intelligence was relocated to the realm of the rhythmic system, man was then only halfway dependent on the hierarchies. Only at the third stage, from the fifteenth century onward, when human beings had become head beings through the third cosmic event, did it became possible for them to venture onto the path of full inner freedom with complete independence from the hierarchies. 'Intelligence becomes their very own intelligence' — in these words Rudolf Steiner sums up the main consequence of this last event (GA 237, 28 July 1924).[14]

20

In this regard, the observation of a human being awakening out of sleep is interesting. For here, the entire above-pictured macrocosmic process is repeated on the microcosmic level. As the 'I' returns from sleep into the body, the above process first occurs through the limbs; in falling asleep, on the other hand, it leaves the physical body through the head. Accurate observation demonstrates that, in the process of awakening, one initially makes unintentional and unconscious movements with hands and feet. Then, only half awake, one begins to feel and differentiate conditions of warmth and light in one's surroundings, something that corresponds to the grasping hold of the rhythmic system on the part of the 'I'. It is, however, only after the 'I' has fully penetrated the head-system, and with that begins to activate thinking, that the process of waking is completely finished.

In the above-quoted lecture, Rudolf Steiner goes on to point out something quite special in connection with the cosmic process he has described. He states that all anthroposophists — if they but look deeply enough into their souls — not only can remember their participation in the instructions within the Michael School, but that at the beginning of that School they were moreover allowed to witness and experience this cosmic tempest around the Earth. And when we are in a position to remember that we have actually experienced this tempest as an expression of the complete alteration of human nature, this recollection can call forth in our soul what we need above all for the further unfolding of anthroposophy on Earth, namely genuine enthusiasm and true spiritual fervour for anthroposophy itself; genuine enthusiasm and true spiritual fervour that is rooted in the supersensible karma that has guided us to anthroposophy on Earth. 'It should be understood, my dear friends, that these lightening flashes, these thunderbolts, are supposed to change into genuine *enthusiasm* in the hearts and minds of anthroposophists!' (ibid.).

One can also formulate this in the opposite way: If today we increasingly run into the fact that less and less enthusiasm for anthroposophy is detected among anthroposophists, that only means that they are no longer in a position to recall this cosmic tempest, and because of that are unable to connect correctly with their Michaelic karma prior to birth. This has actual consequences. For what happened due to this tempest? Human beings have become persons of the head. At the same time, however, we have absorbed the predisposition — even into our physical constitution — for cognizing the spirit quite consciously and freely. Now, this is not a cognizing through external intellectuality, but one where we are able to understand the contents of the spiritual world with our own thinking. And it is for this that our souls were prepared in the Michael School, so that following this schooling process we might find ourselves in a position to penetrate the spiritual world through anthroposophy on Earth by thinking. This signifies that, with their thoughts, such souls can understand not only the world of nature around them, but likewise fully comprehend the processes and entities of the spiritual world. Then, out of this arises spiritual enthusiasm as well — which at the same time is the recollection of what we were allowed to experience once from out of the Sun Sphere as a cosmic event at the beginning of the Michael School in the spiritual world — for a new thought-borne life in spiritual contents.

Now it depends on the karma of a given human being whether he or she can understand spiritual-scientific contents through healthy human reasoning here on Earth or not. And it becomes obvious that it is the participation by a human being in the supersensible Michael School that essentially accounts for this special karma that leads to the comprehension of anthroposophy. For there, through experiencing the preparation for anthroposophy, the karmic foundations were laid into the human being for subsequently comprehending it as well on Earth.[15]

What has just been said is linked with yet another secret of our time. For the comprehension of the spiritual contents of anthroposophy by means of human thinking — something that according to *Occult Science, an Outline* corresponds to the first stage of modern initiation — is only the beginning of the inner path that must be pursued by human beings today in the Michael epoch. The next stage on this path, to which Michael himself would like to lead human beings, is described by Rudolf Steiner as follows. Michael '...liberates the thoughts from the domain of the head; he opens up the way for them to the heart; he loosens enthusiasm from heart and mind so that a human being can live with soul-devotion in regard to everything that can be experienced in *thought-light*. The Michael age has commenced. Hearts are beginning to have thoughts. Enthusiasm no longer streams merely out of mystical darkness but out of thought-borne soul-clarity. To understand this means to receive Michael into one's inmost nature [*Gemüt*] or, put even more precisely, into one's heart' (see *Anthroposophical Leading Thoughts*, 'At the Beginning of the Michael-Age', GA 26, emphasis by Rudolf Steiner). For '...now, human beings who are

23

linked to Michael recognize that they should allow Michael to dwell in their hearts' (ibid.). Just as formerly the souls of anthroposophists lived together with Michael in his supersensible School in the midst of his mighty Sun-domain — in this 'cosmic heart of worlds' — so now, as if in an earthly replica, the opposite must take place. Those human beings who went with Michael must now erect, in the midst of the Earth-domain, the new dwelling place for Michael in the human heart. For '... in the future, Michael wants to set up his seat in the hearts ... of earthly human beings' (GA 240, 21 August 1924).

Likewise, in the above-quoted words that describe the Michaelic path from head to heart-thinking, it is a matter of this new quality of enthusiasm, without which one cannot erect a dwelling place for Michael in one's own heart. This is why, during the laying of the Foundation Stone (on 25 December 1923, GA 260), Rudolf Steiner speaks about the transformation of 'the heart's system of rhythm' into 'the heart as an organ of cognition [*Erkenntnis*],' with which the human being can receive the new cosmic revelations out of the rhythms of worlds in which Michael lives.[16]

In conclusion, as was said before, there is yet another stage on this path where we must learn not only to think in the Michaelic way with the heart (to use the heart as a new organ of cognition), but also to be active on Earth based on these new insights of the heart, to have initiative in life, to become creative out of the cognized spirit. In order to achieve this, we have passed through the third heavenly preparation of anthroposophy before birth, namely through the supersensible cultus where the lofty teachings by the supersensible Michael School were linked with the will of human souls participating in that School.

24

It follows from what was stated above that the great macrocosmic path that was once pursued by humanity—the path on which the First Hierarchy took the thought-substance of the cosmos out of the Sun-realm of the Second Hierarchy and implanted it into the human limb-system on Lemuria, then on Atlantis into the heart-system, and finally at the beginning of the fifteenth century into our head system—this great macrocosmic path must now be pursued in a microcosmic way in the opposite direction by human beings in the light of Michael consciously and freely, namely from the head to the heart and from there into the limb-system.

Summing this up, one can say:

The stages of the celestial preparation of anthroposophy:	$\longrightarrow$	Its main consequences on Earth.
First Hierarchy (Starry Universe)	1. Cosmic Tempest	— Comprehension of anthroposophical communications from the spiritual world.
Second Hierarchy (Sun Sphere)	2. Michael School	— Thinking with the heart (Ether-heart becomes organ of cognition).
Third Hierarchy (Moon Sphere)[17]	3. Michael Cultus	— Becoming creative (taking initiative) on Earth based on spirit-cognition.

And here, when we recall once more that the above described macrocosmic path is at the same time the path on which the individual ego 'lives its way' into the being of man, we will moreover understand this microcosmic path to be the one that leads us from the head, through the heart and limbs, and to the spiritual origin of our 'I', as described in the course through the 19 Class Lessons. For the true being of the 'I' can only be found where the karma of human beings is at work — in the depths of his or her will.

A further significant consequence of the Christmas Conference was the actual founding of the Michael School on Earth. This Michael School was then actually established out of that spirit which had been invoked at the Christmas Conference, so as to imbue the entire anthroposophical movement from then on. Rudolf Steiner spoke of this in looking back on the Christmas Conference, saying: 'We want to work together in such a way — *with the spirit* that was effective at the Christmas Conference — that the actively working impulse of this Christmas Conference may never cease to exist among anthroposophists who strive correctly to recognize the conditions of anthroposophical life ... *The spirit* we attempted to invoke — *this spirit* would always be present through the good will, through the devotion, and through the penetrating comprehension by the members for anthroposophy and anthroposophical life' (GA 260a, 6 February 1924). But it may certainly also be stated that this new spirit, that gradually led to the further development of anthroposophical esotericism, is something that Rudolf Steiner pointed out in the following words: 'It may indeed be noted that a spirit — gradually entering more deeply into the esoteric element — will go through the spiritual life that in turn is to flow through the Anthroposophical Society' (GA 260a, 7 June 1924). And only out of this new spirit could the Michael School then be established on Earth[18] as the esoteric centre of the anthroposophical movement and 'soul of the Anthroposophical Society' (GA 260, 28 December 1923).[19]

This affirms that the Michael School is inseparably united with the esoteric impulse of the Christmas Conference and appears as its direct consequence. This is why it is already mentioned during the Christmas Conference and is included in the statutes that are discussed there and agreed to by the members (§ 5).

For this spirit of the New Mysteries, Rudolf Steiner on occasion also used the more veiled designation, 'esoteric trend',[20] a term that imbued and inwardly formed the Christmas Conference. Yet, at the end of the Foundation Stone laying on 25 December 1923, Rudolf Steiner pointed directly to the presence of this spirit in the entirety of these events: 'And then will you carry *that* spirit, which reigns in the radiant light of thoughts around the dodecahedral Stone of Love, out into the world where it should give of its light and warmth for the progress of human souls; for the progress of the world' (GA 260). Then, during the first report on the Christmas Conference in the *Newsletter*, Rudolf Steiner writes about the Foundation Stone as 'the mental attitude flowing out of the anthroposophical fashioning of life' (GA 260a, 13 January 1924). He describes this attitude as follows: 'In the manner as is demanded by the signs of the present time,[21] this attitude is expressed in the will to find the way — through human soul-deepening — to perception of the spirit and life out of

27

the spirit' (ibid.). And it is precisely to this twofold aim that the School of Spiritual Science would like to lead the modern human being, namely to conscious 'perceiving of the spirit' in the General Section, and to 'living out of the spirit' in the various special sections.

If one looks from this perspective upon the contents of the First Class, one can ascertain that, even though the Class itself signifies a mighty step forward in anthroposophical esotericism and stands simultaneously for a completely new institution, it is at the same time deeply anchored in the mainstream of anthroposophy's evolution. This is confirmed by the following fact. In 1904, Rudolf Steiner began with the publication of articles that in 1909 appeared as the book *Knowledge of the Higher Worlds*. This work ends — and the end is without doubt its culmination — with the description of the spirit-disciple's encounter with the Guardian of the Threshold. If a bridge is now formed to the First Class from the two last chapters of the above book, we find that Rudolf Steiner sets out with the First Lesson, but now on a higher level, precisely where the book *Knowledge of the Higher Worlds* concludes, namely, with the encounter with the Guardian of the Threshold.[22]

Thus, the Guardian becomes the lofty guide of the human soul through ever higher regions of the spiritual world, following this encounter with the spirit disciple in the first Class Lesson. One realizes how one situation passes directly over into another one, and also discovers in them an uninterrupted and consistent further advancement. Within it, the question that must arise for any reader of the above-mentioned book is definitely answered: Now, what happens following this first meeting with the

Guardian? And how does the spirit-disciple's life continue on after this first encounter?

Here, anthroposophy is in a completely unique position today in the midst of the most varied spiritual movements of the present age. As far as I can evaluate this, it is only in anthroposophy that a modern human being can find so much fundamental and decisive information about the Threshold to the spiritual world and its Guardian. In the world today we have countless numbers of paths, each alleging to lead into the spiritual world: older and newer ones, Christian and Eastern ones, simple and complicated ones. But what distinguishes anthroposophy so fundamentally from all other movements is the fact that it is the only spiritual movement that researches the domain of the Threshold in such magnitude, depth and thoroughness, as well as the entire subject-matter of the Guardian, and then makes it available to human beings. (It naturally goes without saying that there are still further differences.) And if one has sufficient courage to think this set of circumstances all the way through, this signifies nothing less than the recognition that today it is *only* the anthroposophical path of schooling that is able to lead the human being to the Threshold and then in full consciousness past the Guardian into the spiritual world. In the case of other spiritual streams, this does not occur at all. It follows from this that practically all of them seek to penetrate into the spiritual world while circumventing the Threshold.

Here, precisely, the weighty question arises: What consequences does this entail for countless souls that today attempt to enter the spiritual world, and even get in without any knowledge of the Threshold? Without any conscious experience of the Threshold, one cannot discern what kind of fundamental, basic differences exist there between the world around us and the world beyond. For if one does not pass with full consciousness through the decisive metamorphosis of one's whole being at the Threshold, one is not in a position to distinguish between reality, illusion and deception in the spiritual world. Then one will much more easily become a play-thing for the powers whose true nature one can no longer see through.

It is only on the basis of genuine knowledge of the secrets of the Threshold that justified entrance into the spiritual world occurs today. And only thereby can one find the strength within oneself to tolerate and overcome the decisive metamorphosis of one's own being at the Threshold. In particular, the last chapters of the book *Knowledge of the Higher Worlds* attest to the fact that this metamorphosis is most dramatic, even shattering, in its nature. It even says there that these Threshold-experiences are of a kind that the human being cannot tolerate without careful preparation. It says, for instance, concerning the encounter with the Lesser Guardian, that: 'Without due preparation nobody could indeed tolerate the view of things indicated here' (GA 10). And in *Occult Science, an Outline* it says in regard to the encounter with the Greater Guardian: 'If through an improper spirit-discipline one would approach this experience unprepared, something would then pour ... into the soul that can only be compared with a "feeling of immeasurable terror", a "boundless fear"' (GA 13).

From what is said here, the danger likewise becomes discernible to which an unprepared soul can succumb if it makes the attempt to enter into the spiritual world without having experienced both an earlier awakening at the

Threshold and the encounter with the Guardian. Now, when this does in fact happen, one hears from such unprepared people how they perceive and describe the spiritual world as being quite similar to the earthly one. While everything becomes in some way more thinned down and tenuous in substance, a bit more moral and light-filled, it remains too closely related to the physical world to be the true spiritual world. In this way, one does not escape a delicate subtle materialism that merely becomes veiled and occult. Or, one becomes caught up in a sphere of experiences resembling dreams, which increasingly threatens one's inner autonomy and free will, ultimately endangering one to become bound up with the so-called Eighth or Evil Sphere.[23]

Now, the problem of the Threshold is connected with something that has even greater significance, and that is in fact true for all human beings. According to Rudolf Steiner's spirit-research, around the middle of the nineteenth century humanity unconsciously crossed over the Threshold of the spiritual world. He even names a precise point in time for this — the years from 1842 to 1879. This is also the time when Michael had to wage his battle against certain ahrimanic spirits in order to take up his position as leading Time Spirit in humanity's evolution. Thus, these two events fall within the same time-span: In his battle against the Spirits of Darkness, Michael purified that very spiritual sphere beyond the Threshold into which humanity entered unconsciously around the same time. (This profound theme can be touched upon here only in passing.)

As a result, the whole of humankind has lived beyond the Threshold for more than 100 years already, but in

31

general has no awareness, not even an inkling of this at all. This is why one of the most important spiritual tasks of our time — to look back in retrospection on this, having already crossed over the Threshold, as it were — consists of increasingly becoming aware of it. This is why it is likewise a matter of calling forth the Michaelic courage at the Threshold so as consciously to encounter the World Abyss and the stern Guardian who stands there. For, if this set of facts continues to be ignored by human beings and remains without consequences, still uncountable catastrophes will break in upon humanity.

Rudolf Steiner sums up this situation in the following words: 'In the forties of the nineteenth century, these matters were basically lost [referring to the last traces of ancient spiritual wisdom]. The abyss is there until the end of the nineteenth century where, due to the Michael age, these matters can be found again [the new linking up of human beings to the spiritual world as a result of the Michael call]. Then, however, as human beings crossed over this abyss, they in a sense stepped over a threshold, and a Guardian stands at this Threshold. Initially, humanity could not simultaneously pay heed to him inasmuch as they went past him between the years 1842 and 1879. But for their own sake, human beings must now look back and take notice of the Guardian. For not paying heed and just going on living [as before] into the following centuries without listening to him would indeed lead to the most extreme catastrophe for humankind' (GA 233a, 12 January 1924).

In other words: If such awareness of the Threshold does not take place in a free and conscious way, then — because there is no awareness of the spiritual world — not the good spiritual powers but above all the evil ones will sneak out of the spiritual world into the sub-consciousness of human beings and do their mischief, whereby human beings would fall prey to demonic entities. Particularly today, following all the horrendous experiences of the twentieth century, during which the largest variety of new forms of formerly unthinkable evil surfaced, one can seriously ask oneself whether all human beings have not already been connected with the above described situation. Only the awakening at the Threshold and a conscious encounter with the Guardian can change this fatal situation and save mankind from still greater catastrophes. This is the second reason why the epochal cognitional breakthrough of anthroposophy in the domain of the Threshold is of decisive significance for the present and for the future.

Correct perception of the Threshold in our time is of central importance for three more reasons. For only based on this insight can the present appearance of the Christ in the etheric be truly experienced and understood. And this is precisely because His etheric Second Coming occurs today at the Threshold to the spiritual world.

The second reason is connected with the main task of the Fifth Post-Atlantean epoch, the task consisting in the knowledge of evil and the effect of the opposing powers in humanity's evolution. At the eve of the incarnation of Ahriman on Earth, this knowledge is extremely important and inseparable from the secret of the Threshold, for it is only at this Threshold that the true intentions of the opposing powers can actually be recognized.[24] This secret of humanity's evolution was summed up by Rudolf Steiner in the following verse for Ita Wegman:

There, where the Light
Flickers
In front of green demons,
And the light-born
Primordial cosmic forces
Annunciate
To struggling human beings
The riddles
That can only be enticed
From the demons
By human beings
And then can be brought
To gods
Soul found the soul
So that one day to sacrifice
To waiting gods
The secret of demons
At region of darkness —
That light it may become
Where without this deed
Eternal darkness held sway.
Such a place exists
It must disappear
Cause it eventually to disappear.
Thus speaks admonishingly
Michael's glance.[25]

The third reason is that, beginning in our time, it is only
through consciously crossing over the Threshold that
human beings can altogether perceive and retain their
own 'I' in the spiritual world. Otherwise, during their
further ascent into higher worlds, they would at best end

up only in ecstasy (Samadhi) that extinguishes any individual 'I'-consciousness. Although they would arrive at spiritual experience, they would lose themselves completely in so doing, meaning they would cease to be 'I'-endowed human beings.

This is why, when the actual *crossing of the Threshold occurs* on the path of the 19 Class Lessons, the ancient primal words resound that, through all ages, challenge us to take hold of our true being.

For without this Threshold-experience, true self-knowledge of man that becomes world-knowledge, and with that leads to knowledge of the spiritual world, is in no way possible.

The three most important experiences of the present-day human being at the Threshold are therefore:

— The encounter with the Etheric Christ
— The recognition of evil
— The self-knowledge of the human being which leads to true knowledge of the spiritual world

When we summarize the inner connection of these two major esoteric consequences of the Christmas Conference, it can be expressed as follows. If one recognizes in the karma lectures — above all in their culmination inherent in the communications concerning the three stages of the heavenly preparation of anthroposophy — a sort of goal of inner striving as faithful Michael disciples, namely the possibility to link up consciously with one's own Michaelic and cosmic karma here on Earth, then the mantric content of the First Class forms the actual path on which this goal can be realized in practical terms. What was once an event of the spiritual world (the supersensible

Michael School), will as a result of our free efforts find its continuation on Earth so that humankind will in due course have fulfilled their task in the Michaelic sense.

The third main consequence of the Christmas Conference is the second Goetheanum building. In this depiction, reference can only be made to that aspect of this deed by Rudolf Steiner which is linked primarily with the secret of the Threshold. The first Goetheanum, that brought anthroposophy to expression as a visible imagination, was originally conceived in such a way that it was not supposed to have any outward formation. It was intended to be built like a rock-temple or subterranean temple. Only because it was nevertheless supposed to stand openly within the landscape, for reasons not connected directly with the original intention, its outer *gestalt* or form was likewise developed.

Due to the fire on the night of New Year's Eve 1922, all its forms and colours that had been brought to visible expression as living anthroposophy entered into the spiritual world, into the 'wide etheric world where the spirit lives', or put more precisely, in which 'lives the spirit-filled Wisdom [Sophia] of the universe' (GA 233a, 22 April 1924). In this way, a matter that originally was part of and belonged with the Earth became an affair of the spiritual cosmos, i.e., it lived on as spirit in the ether-worlds of that spiritual cosmos.

In accordance with the lecture of 13 January 1924 (GA 233a), one can say that it was Michael himself who received this free deed of human beings (the structure) into the spiritual world, so that 'as the good spirit of the Goetheanum' (GA 260, 'On Behalf of the Members'), having been received once more by Rudolf Steiner from

36

the spiritual world, it would continue to work and be effective among human beings as the new 'esoteric trend'.

It is out of this spirit that Rudolf Steiner then forms the entire esoteric content of the Christmas Conference. In the Conference itself, a report was given on the Goetheanum's reconstruction (already announced during a lecture on 31 December 1923, GA 260) and the architectural principles guiding it. On the last day of the Christmas Conference, Rudolf Steiner adds to this: '... what has happened here — I know it — I was allowed to say it — for it was said in full responsibility looking up to the spirit who is there and who should be and will be the spirit of the Goetheanum' (GA 260, 'On Behalf of the Members').

Just a few months later, Rudolf Steiner fashions the model of the second Goetheanum in plasticine, taking as a basis a completely different principle of structure from the first building. In it, everything was formed from the inner space in the way the human soul experiences the secrets of the cosmos in connection with its own being. In the second building, on the other hand, the formative forces came completely from outside out of the widths of the cosmos — one can also say, out of Michael's kingdom itself — where now the spirit of the Goetheanum was to be found.[26] From there, Rudolf Steiner received them during the Christmas Conference: 'The Goetheanum was carried up and out into the cosmos [through the conflagration] and we can permeate ourselves by the Goetheanum impulses that come in from the cosmos' (GA 233a, 22 April 1924). In other words: Out of the Goetheanum's spirit working from the cosmos, the model was created for the second structure. And in its forms, the impulses of the Christmas Conference were likewise brought directly to expression in an artistic manner. This is why Rudolf Steiner said, already during the Christmas Conference, that the forms of the concrete structure 'can offer *something new* to artistic observation', and that in comparison with the 'old Goetheanum-forms ... [the new] concrete forms ... *have to be completely different'* (GA 260, 31 December 1923).

The entirety represents a grand metamorphosis. What had been transformed out of inner experiences of the soul on the modern path of initiation into an artistic work (first Goetheanum) moved as human deed into the widths of the etheric cosmos in order, from there, to be infused by cosmic wisdom in the realm of Michael; to return again as a purely spiritual impulse — from which Rudolf Steiner formed the second structure as a 'Michael Castle'[27] that stands unshakably on the first one. What had been inner space before, now appeared out of the etheric–universal all as cosmic force; force that is effective all the way even into solid matter, giving visible form to the latter. In this transformation of the inner into the outer, during the passage from the first to the second Goetheanum, we have the central experience of the human soul at the Threshold. What previously had made up the content of inner life now appears at the Threshold objectively mirrored as an approaching new reality out of the spiritual world. This fundamental experience by the human being at the Threshold to the spiritual world was brought to expression by Rudolf Steiner in the metamorphosis of the forms from the first Goetheanum to the second one. And in this sense, the forms of the second Goetheanum must be internalized and experienced meditatively by the modern human being as a threshold-experience that is gradually becoming perceptible.

A further secret resulting from the relationship between the forms of the second Goetheanum and the karma lectures should be touched upon briefly here. Let us recall first that with the artistic configuration, not only of the first Goetheanum but in particular of the second one, Rudolf Steiner created 'completely new [plastic, architectonic] forms awakening karma perception' (GA 236, 27 April 1924), the origins of which were accompanied by the karma lectures of the year 1924. Thus we discover in the area of karma a new correlation of what lived in the Rosicrucian schools from the very beginning as the nurturing of both principles: a clairvoyant state and initiation. 'This specific mission — to create a balance between the principles of clairvoyance and initiation — approached the leading powers of mankind in recent times. As a matter of necessity, leaders of spiritual discipline had to focus on what is referred to here with the beginning of the modern age. The particular esoteric direction that fits the present time — meaning that Rosicrucian stream which takes its direction from the Michael impulse — in principle always brings about the correct relationship between clairvoyance and initiation' (GA 15, Chapter II). One can say: If the forms of the second structure were to lead to the *perception* of karma (clairvoyant principle), the karma lectures have the task of guiding the human being to the insights belonging with the aforementioned lectures (initiation principle).

These two principles were then led to a further, still higher, synthesis in the First Class of the School of Spiritual Science, and transformed into the possibility consciously to work on the karma of the Anthroposophical Society as a new karma-community in the Michaelic sense, which means based on *true insight of the ego-being*.[28] One can also say: In the then still to be erected 'Michael Castle', human beings who are called upon to do so were, in full consciousness, to recognize their prenatal Michaelic karma, so as to become spiritual co-workers in the First Class of the Time Spirit on the modern path of initiation.

*

Let us return to the question posed at the outset. From whom does the third call actually proceed that resounds through the entire Christmas Conference? What being of the spiritual world works there at the behest of Michael and directs his call to all of us through Rudolf Steiner's mediation? In order to answer this question, let us look once again at the two pillars of the anthroposophical path of schooling, pillars that are most strongly connected with the nature of the Threshold — the book *Knowledge of the Higher Worlds* (the corresponding passages from *Occult Science, an Outline* are part of it too) and the contents of the First Class.[29] From such a consideration, the following results. Between these two basic pillars, there exists yet another special connecting link as a spiritual bridge, and this is the final lecture of the Christmas Conference that Rudolf Steiner gave in the evening of the first day of New Year 1924. In it he gave a clear and unambiguous reply to the posed question. This is why much depends on whether we are willing to take this reply seriously enough and moreover to evoke the courage to think through what Rudolf Steiner communicated to the very end, so that this circumstance will reveal itself to us in its awe-inspiring consequence. For it is in no way theoretical, but directly concerns the whole future of the anthroposophical movement on Earth.

The above-mentioned lecture deals primarily with the encounter with the Guardian, as well as with our great responsibility regarding the contemporary situation of humanity at the Threshold. In this respect it is also note-worthy that there is hardly any other lecture in Rudolf Steiner's entire work (with the exception of his address to the Russians),[30] where he uses the word *responsibility* as much. On the occasion of its first publication, this is why Marie Steiner gave this lecture the title, 'The Proper Entry into the Spiritual World. The Responsibility Placed Upon Us' (GA 260).

First, the lecture contains a description of what the modern initiate experiences at the threshold to the spiritual world as the highest dramatic situation of humankind in our age. Countless human souls who have passed through today's education and lifestyle — and as a result are in all their thoughts and feelings burdened due to present-day civilization in the materialistic sense — appear every night at the Threshold before the stern Guardian after falling asleep. He, however, does not allow them into the spiritual world because that world cannot tolerate the materialistic character of contemporary civi-lization. If these souls could nevertheless cross over the Threshold, beyond it they would become paralysed, and along with the subsequent awakening would gradually lose the ability to think at all on Earth. For their own protection, therefore, the Guardian denies them entry into the spiritual world.

A further tragedy inherent in this situation is that the Guardian can deny these human souls entry into the spiritual world only during their sleep, whereby the above-described danger is averted *only for a certain time*. After death, on the other hand, the Guardian cannot cause these souls to stay indefinitely in the surroundings of the Earth. In time he will have to grant them access into the higher spheres, for otherwise they could not prepare their next incarnation properly. As a result of the inner paralysis that occurs, they appear in the next Earth-life in such a way that they will be less and less able to think on Earth. Such souls will then above all be guided by feelings, urges, instincts and emotions, something that can be observed increasingly in the world today and confirms that the described situation remains most acute in its further perspective.

At this point we must ask in all seriousness: What does it actually imply that mankind will in this way gradually unlearn thinking? We know from various results of spirit research by Rudolf Steiner how today's independent thinking in the human being originated through the fact that Michael's cosmic intelligence has departed the lofty Sun Sphere after the Mystery of Golgotha, and in the following centuries has sunk down into human souls. Then, however, along with the beginning of the consciousness soul epoch on Earth, it increasingly became the most important destiny-question between Michael and Ahriman: Which one of the two will ultimately have this intelligence in his possession? For after the ninth century in the kingdom of human beings, Michael no longer had any direct access to the cosmic intelligence that had slipped from him. This is why he waits for human beings to return it to him based on their own freedom meaning that they will create the conditions through which Michael can once more unite with it. And 'the hearts [of human beings] must become Michael's helpers in the regaining of the intelligence that has fallen from heaven to the Earth' (GA 240, 20 July 1924). For only in this way can a human being today attain free and conscious entry into the spiritual world.

In the situation that has arisen, Ahriman on the other hand sees the unique opportunity ultimately to guide the intelligence that has separated from Michael into his domain of power and with it to push all of Earth evolution into those directions that correspond solely to his nature and goals. Now, if it were to happen that humanity would cease from thinking in the way described, in doing so they would leave the fallow-lying intelligence 'voluntarily' to Ahriman and would thus assure his authority over the on-going Earth evolution. So that this will not come to pass, the Michael School exists on Earth. For by its very nature it is destined to work against the impulses that arise today in humanity's evolution from the subterranean Ahriman School.[31] For the ahrimanic danger is extraordinarily powerful in our time, and human thinking is most parti-cularly exposed to it. People lose the faculty to grasp the spiritual with their thinking.[32]

Now, to this one might perhaps respond that Rudolf Steiner stated this over 80 years ago based on his obser-vations at the Threshold; today it may be completely dif-ferent. But what is it like in actuality in our time? Here I would like to raise the notion that this situation has meanwhile become even more crucial, notwithstanding many new occult and spiritual streams that have since proliferated, and supposedly are testimony to an ever-increasing overcoming of materialism. For in reality

43

materialism, as the greatest evil of our time, has not disappeared at all. It has merely passed through a metamorphosis that makes it even more powerful and underhand. The oldest so-called theoretical materialism of the nineteenth century was in a certain regard still the most harmless, for as yet it almost did not concern the deeper layers of human nature at all. It remained predominantly an abstract, purely intellectual ideology, a sort of fabrication by the head.

At this point, one may perhaps recall that, precisely in reference to this theoretical materialism, Rudolf Steiner, in his book *The Course of My Life*, submits the example of two so-called 'unknown acquaintances', two souls that he could trace in their existence following death after an Earth-life in which they had completely submerged themselves in the then prevalent theoretical materialism. Based on spiritual-scientific observations, it became clear that relatively soon after death they had overcome their theoretical materialism (GA 28, Chap. XX). In this sense theoretical materialism was still relatively harmless.

Then, in the twentieth century, and particularly after World War II, materialism ceased to be primarily an ideology and increasingly became the new standard of living for countless human beings within the domain of Western civilization. There arose the so-called 'consumer-society' whose protagonists may even still have gone to church on Sundays, but day by day lived as pure materialists; something that, viewed spiritually, is even worse than theoretical materialism which by now has died out to a large extent.

In this life of materialism, where one might even entertain all kinds of splendid ideals in one's head but in reality lives as if materialism were the only truth, a frightening aphorism by Rudolf Steiner comes to mind. In it he once brought to expression that it is self-evident that materialism in accordance with its very nature is false; however, in humanity's evolution the real danger exists that one day it will become true as a reality of life.

Then there is yet another, third, stage. It started at the end of the twentieth century and will continue on into the twenty-first century and far beyond it. It consists of the following. Materialism itself will assume an occult character and will thereby be disguised even better in its outward appearance. For today, this materialistic ideology pushes more and more strongly into the spiritual world — because humankind knows nothing of the earlier-described crossing over the Threshold — so that conceptions about it become increasingly materialistic. As a result, the spiritual world is frequently depicted more and more as if it was basically no different from the physical sense world, and in fact only represents a refined and tenuous copy. This is the principal idea of numerous New Age movements. While they originated in the last century, in this one they will acquire a much greater power and prevalence within humanity than ever before. Elsewhere it has been described by me in detail[33] how in such occult streams the spiritual world is viewed in such a way that one finds in it occult atoms, occult electricity, as well as all kinds of force and energy fields, plus other characteristics of the physical sense world. What was still represented in the twentieth century as new occult 'teachings' by a few 'select gurus' will become 'spiritual' experiences of an ever larger number of human beings. And because in their often quite sincere striving toward the spiritual world they hear nothing of the Threshold, the spiritual world as they conceive it becomes filled through Ahriman's power with the qualities of the physical world.[34] And furthermore, this just described tendency is found today not only in New Age movements but increasingly in the perceptions of existing denominations.

Here, just one example: Embarrassed, one either avoids speaking of angels at all or one 'speaks' of them as if one were dealing with humanoid beings that one might encounter like a good friend. Lacking comprehensive knowledge of the Threshold in all this, it can in no way be noticed at all what a powerful metamorphosis occurs in and with human beings when they would like to take the actual step from earthly consciousness to a very first inkling [*Ahnung*] of what an angelic consciousness might be like, not to mention an angel itself. Many more examples could be indicated here from newer religious or occult literature, something that would not fit into the framework of this depiction. One thing, however, is certain: One does not speak with angels as simply as one does during a 'five o'clock tea'. In actuality this does not work. But it does work relatively simply with the various kinds of counterforces that can assume even the form of all sorts of 'light-beings',[35] when seen through the 'eyes' of the unsuspecting 'clairvoyant'.

In the lecture of 1 January 1924, having characterized this dramatic situation of humanity at the Threshold, Rudolf Steiner begins to mention something that — if one would merely listen to it superficially — could even mislead anthroposophists to a certain arrogance. If on the contrary one understands it properly, it should lead to the point where one can only feel ashamed as an anthro-

46

posophist. One only needs to take what Rudolf Steiner says in the context of the whole Christmas Conference, where those members who were present heard the Foundation Stone verse which began each morning for nine days with the threefold call 'Soul of Man'. Now, at the end of the lecture, hence at the end of the conference, Rudolf Steiner speaks of the fact that anthroposophical souls will hear something completely different from what ordinary human souls would have heard as the stern reply by the Guardian of the Threshold: 'For your own sake, you may not cross over the Threshold; you may not gain access into the spiritual world; you must go back' (GA 260) for otherwise you will become 'paralysed in your soul' (ibid.). It is of utmost importance that one takes these words as seriously as possible; words that are actually directed to us as anthroposophists by the Guardian himself.

It is a matter of two short sentences that Rudolf Steiner reiterates, however, as the Guardian's straightforward message, sentences that he directs to anthroposophical souls every night when they appear in sleep at the Threshold to the spiritual world. From this emerges the decisive question as to whether we hear these words by the Guardian in order to convert them subsequently into concrete actions, or whether we want to sleep through them, as happens constantly in 'countless cases' (ibid.) among our contemporaries. These two short sentences are actually two statements by the Guardian that Rudolf Steiner transmits one after the other. First the Guardian says to *us*: 'In order to hear the voice out of spirit land, thou must develop the powerful courage to testify [*sich bekennen*] to this voice, for thou hast begun to be awake; courage will keep thee awake' (ibid).

Here, one must call to mind once more the entire situation. A mighty call that is repeated every day passes through the whole Christmas Conference. But now, at the end of the Conference, an answer is given to the question of who it actually is that calls out to human beings during the nine days. The answer is: the Guardian himself out of the realm of the Threshold. And at this point no further insights are demanded of the anthroposophists, only strong courage. There, Rudolf Steiner even uses words he otherwise does not use frequently: 'to testify to'. To take this voice, that powerfully resounded through the entire Christmas Conference, and to relate it to oneself personally, like a call out of spirit land, and to represent it decisively in one's life — that requires true courage.

If one finds this courage in one's self, one confesses with this courage that the esoteric impulse of the Christmas Conference was simultaneously a mighty call out of the domain of the Threshold; a call that proceeds from the Guardian. And if one furthermore demonstrates the willingness courageously to admit to his voice, then one gradually begins to awaken on the Threshold. 'For thou hast begun to awaken!'

It is also striking how the above-mentioned three stages that Rudolf Steiner describes in the introduction to the first rhythm (26 December 1923) correspond to the content of this last lecture in which the Guardian himself speaks. Here too it is a matter of an intensified *responsibility* in regard to the voice one has heard from the spiritual world, and the will *to follow* this voice in order then to *pervade* oneself with it — meaning to side with this voice without compromise; that is, courageously to testify to it and stand up for it. Unshakeable devotion to the Christmas Conference is addressed with this.[36]

According to Rudolf Steiner's spirit research, countless numbers of contemporary souls exist today in deep sleep at the Threshold to the spiritual world. On the other hand, because anthroposophists have heard the Guardian's resounding voice, and if they now have the courage to stand up for this voice, they have thereby been given the unique opportunity to awaken at the Threshold. If that happens, they may hear the second admonition by the Guardian of the Threshold once again in direct words, mediated through Rudolf Steiner: 'The only point that remains is that you should still be tested regarding your courage to testify to what you can obviously hear as a voice through the inclination of your *Gemüt*, through the inclination of your heart and mind' (ibid.).[37] This means, one can consciously develop *an inclination of the heart* to hear this voice. And the heart is the place wherein the human being can implant the spiritual Foundation Stone for the General Anthroposophical Society.[38] The one thing is that we must not consider these matters in an isolated way but comprehend them in the overall context of the Christmas Conference.

The anthroposophists who during the Christmas Conference have sought and found an inner relationship to the Foundation Stone — and this is to begin with purely an affair of heart-knowledge,[39] for it is the Foundation Stone of *Love* — could in this way develop a kind of 'clair-audience' for the call by the Guardian in the Foundation Stone Meditation, a meditation that accurately describes this Foundation Stone in the form of mantric words, and at the same time bestows a protective shield for it in the hearts of human beings.

The essence of the second statement by the Guardian is that those anthroposophists who of their own free will profess to this voice out of spirit land are still to be put to the test. To be tested in what? The Guardian himself gives answer to this: they must be tested in their courage to own up to what they have clearly heard as the voice through the inclination of their heart. Here, three motives are as if woven together. First, the possibility to hear the voice — for that the entire esoteric content of the Christmas Conference exists. As a reply to this voice, the courage to profess to it — meaning to become a representative of this voice in one's own life. And finally, the possibility gradually to arrive at and awaken in the domain of the Threshold when we actually summon up this courage. With that, as if carrying out a mission for humanity, we can do for human beings what they as yet cannot do for themselves in the present. This means to perceive in spiritual retrospection that, as a human being, each one of us has long since crossed the Threshold to the spiritual world. Now, the stern admonishing Guardian stands at this Threshold, for he needs human beings today who are willing to hear his call. He needs those who summon up the courage to profess to this call and in this way make the resolve to awaken at the Threshold. In this passage, Rudolf Steiner formulates the Guardian's words most precisely: 'For you have begun to awaken'; and that means that you have made the free resolve to move your inner development in the direction of the Threshold where one can ever more awaken, because in this lies the most burning and most necessary task of contemporary humanity.

Yet, the just-described process is still merely the first step to the full awakening at the Threshold. It is first of all only the expression of the will to want to venture forth on this new path, or it is a kind of free promise given to the Guardian really to follow his call. The actual implementation of this resolve, and with that the ultimate awakening at the Threshold, must yet be carried out as a continuation of the new 'esoteric trend' that has proceeded from the Christmas Conference. This is why, if one wishes to continue on this path — and in this actually consists the professing of oneself to the call of the Guardian — this path then leads directly *into the First Class*, which begins already in the first lesson with the situation at the Threshold. For in the path through the 19 Class Lessons, a mantricly formulated possibility is given us to become fully awake at the Threshold to the spiritual world.

We can therefore say: In the concluding lecture of the Christmas Conference — in which the Foundation Stone Meditation also resounded for the first time in the sequence of its parts in the way we are allowed to receive this meditation into our meditative life since the conference — we not only have the transition from the book *Knowledge of the Higher Worlds* to the First Class; the content of this lecture also shows us where the actual impulse must be sought in ourselves so that we may become members of the First Class. The reasons for joining lie precisely in what is pointed out in this lecture. As said before, every night countless human souls come to the Threshold of the spiritual world and there hear the stern rejecting words by the Guardian. Then, among these countless souls we find souls of anthroposophists —

although as yet only very few — who, through 'a grace of karma' in Rudolf Steiner's words, have found anthroposophy in their life,[40] and therefore can gradually begin to awaken at the Threshold. The decision for awakening is, however, connected with the esoteric essence of the Christmas Conference, namely with the moment when we have heard the voice of the Guardian and have summoned up the courage unfalteringly to stand by this voice. Nevertheless, what has been said represents only the very starting point of a long journey. Yet even the first step in that direction is of decisive importance in our time — inasmuch as one makes a decision — in view of the earnest countenance of the stern Guardian that introduces and determines all further steps.

From what was stated, an additional significance of the Christmas Conference's esoteric impulse (as well as the 'esoteric trend' proceeding from it) becomes evident; a trend that, according to Rudolf Steiner's words since then, must pervade the whole anthroposophical movement. For it connects us directly with the Guardian of the Threshold, and for that reason with the most pressing tasks facing humanity in the present time and immediate future.

The actual path to full awakening at the Threshold lies therefore in the First Class, in the spiritual organism of the 19 Lessons. Rudolf Steiner was allowed to receive the mantras directly from the Guardian — whom he describes 'as the ministering member of the Michael power' — so as to pass them along to the members of the Michael School who are entitled to receive them.

The starting point of this path, as already stated, is found in the Christmas Conference, and in its esotericism we likewise find the spiritual roots for our decision to become members of the First Class. For it is the esoteric impulse of the Christmas Conference that allows us even to hear the voice of the Guardian. And when one hears at times among anthroposophists that they are not aware of this voice, i.e., that they cannot recall it in the morning, this is only the result of their not having understood and received the true impulse of the Christmas Conference with sufficient force and intensity as yet. For, every night, when we as appear at the Threshold, we do in fact hear these words from the Guardian that are linked with the challenge to have courage and to profess to his admonition from the spiritual world. Again having returned to day-consciousness, we can freely decide whether we wish to heed or not to heed this call by the Guardian. Then, however, this decision is inseparably connected with our relationship to the Christmas Conference, meaning, as expressed in Rudolf Steiner's words, whether − in our anthroposophical life − this Conference 'is nothing or everything' (GA 260a, 6 February 1924).

In this sense, the decision for membership in the First Class is something definitely real. Its origin is the awakened memory of what we experience in sleep at the Threshold of the spiritual world while standing in front of the Guardian. At the same time, this decision is inseparably linked with the awakened sense of responsibility for the tragic situation of present-day humanity at the Threshold, a condition that Rudolf Steiner described in the last lecture of the Christmas Conference. One can therefore say: This call of the Christmas Conference comes from the Guardian himself, and when we muster the courage to follow it, then obedience to this call leads us into the First Class of the Michael School where, 'at Michael's behest',

53

the Guardian becomes our guide in the spiritual world. For just as Michael speaks to us in the Class Lessons through the Guardian of the Threshold, so the Guardian, likewise at the behest of Michael, turns to us with his call during the Christmas Conference.

As we already saw, the second call to anthroposophists by the Guardian contains the passage, '[the only thing is that] you should still be tested'. One can have diverse thoughts about what might be meant here by a 'test'. Yet it seems obvious that in this case it is above all a matter of the inner relationship to the once understood spirit impulse, a kind of spiritual devotion regarding the freely attained commitment to the voice one has heard from the spiritual world. This is why, during acceptances into the Class in September 1924, Rudolf Steiner said to each candidate quite personally, and looking him or her straight in the eyes: 'If you wish to remain faithful to the Michael School [the First Class], give me your hand.'[41]

It is possible, however, to figure out the nature of this test in a much more concrete way and thereby describe more accurately what is meant by the words 'still be tested'. For the content of the School of Spiritual Science originates directly from the supersensible Michael School. There, in this supersensible School, they were transmitted for the *first* time. Then they were given, in the First Class on Earth, to human beings for the *second* time. It goes without saying that the totality of anthroposophy springs from this cosmic fountainhead, and this is why Rudolf Steiner could once say that the whole of 'the science of spiritual knowledge', as established by him and developed further and further, was 'the gift of Michael' (GA 152, 2 May 1913).

Between general anthroposophy and the contents of the School of Spiritual Science there is, however, one decisive difference. In an article for non-members of the Class, but so as to instruct them about the nature of the Michael School, Rudolf Steiner points out that 'generally, it will therefore have to be like this; namely that the human being will first have to become acquainted with the spiritual world in the form of ideas. Spirit science will be cultivated in this form in the General Anthroposophical Society. There will, however, be personalities who wish to participate in the descriptions of the spiritual world, and they will move upwards from the form of ideas to forms of expression that are borrowed from the spiritual world itself. And others will also be found who want to become acquainted with the paths into the spiritual world in order to move ahead on them with their own soul. For such personalities, there will be the three Classes of the "School". There the efforts, increasingly progressing upwards, will reach up to ever higher degrees of esotericism. The "School" shall guide the participant upwards into those realms of the spiritual world *that cannot be revealed through the form of ideas*. In them the necessity arises to find means of expressions for imaginations, inspirations and intuitions.' (GA 260a, 20 January 1924).

Anthroposophy itself is given to human beings on Earth through the mediation of thinking in the exact form of ideas. With that anthroposophy, in accordance with its nature, is connected with the essential character of our present-day consciousness soul epoch. Its actual source, however, lies in the spiritual world, and that means anthroposophy originally comes out of the world of imaginations, inspirations, and intuitions. And due to the fact that it is put into thought forms, into words, anthroposophy was, from the beginning, inwardly as if surrounded by a sheath and protected that way. (This is why, following the Christmas Conference, Rudolf Steiner could release all lectures to members for publication.)

Rudolf Steiner always spoke in a completely different way and much more sternly about the contents of the School of Spiritual Science. In the above-quoted article, he wrote that an esoteric institution must exist in the anthroposophical movement in which human beings can approach the contents of the spiritual world in a much more direct way. These contents were not to be given primarily through thinking, but directly through imaginations, inspirations and intuitions. So as not to see a contradiction here, this has to be considered a little more closely. Even though the Class Lessons' contents are likewise borne by thoughts, as to their nature and purpose they represent something completely different than the lectures to members. For in the Class Lessons, the substance from the supersensible Michael School comes for the first time out of the spiritual world in such a direct way as was not possible earlier to transmit, even for Rudolf Steiner himself. This is why Rudolf Steiner points out repeatedly in the Class Lessons that inasmuch as the mantric words form their innermost essence, they are the words of Michael himself.

Concerning the karma lectures that were given parallel to the Class Lessons, Rudolf Steiner says that their contents had been known to him already earlier, but that previously he could not speak of them because certain ahrimanic demons had thwarted him from doing so. Only through the spirit impulse of the Christmas Conference were these demons silenced (see GA 240, 12 August 1924). And this victory had the consequence that the karma lectures and also the contents of the Michael School — without their protective thought-sheath — could be given to human beings as directly as Rudolf Steiner formulates this in the last Class Lesson. This set of facts has decisive consequences for us in so far as we are karmicly connected with the anthroposophical stream and understand ourselves to be true Michael students on Earth. Truly, here — one would like to say — the sacred substance of the Michael School has been entrusted for the first time to human beings on Earth. What made up the three stages of the heavenly preparation of anthroposophy with the supersensible Michael School as its very centre, now begins to become full reality on Earth. From then on, this spiritual substance was to be found amongst human beings themselves.

What does this new set of facts demand of us? The Michaelic substance needs our protection; it requires a sheath that only we as true disciples of Michael can give to it in our souls individually and as a human community destined for this. Here, it can become evident without a trace of self-deception how in actuality each one of us stands in relation to Michael by asking, am I only quite generally (meaning in an abstract, hence illusory sense) his pupil, or have I taken his impulse into myself in such a way that I would want to stand up unflinchingly for this Michaelic substance? Do I really experience myself as someone who through his/her karma is called upon, in all humility but quite actually, to be a guardian and caretaker of this substance, so that at least in my soul it can be guarded and nurtured in the way it corresponds to its nature? Only based on my concrete relationship to this Michaelic substance can I truly recognize whether or not, before my birth, I actually was in the Michael School within the holy region of the Sun — from which at the Turning Point of Time Christ came to the Earth — and where I also experienced that cosmic tempest. For in this supersensible Michael School before the countenance of Michael, of my own free will I took upon myself the firm obligation to return to Earth, and there, unselfishly and devotedly, to care for this Michaelic substance.[42] I do so first in my own soul, but then together with all human beings who likewise were in the supersensible Michael School and now as rightful members of the School of Spiritual Science, have recognized their duty in this regard and wish to fulfil it.

This is what the initially puzzling statement by the Guardian signifies, 'You should still be tested'; these words that stand in a direct relationship to his first statement, 'For you have begun to awaken'. First one *begins* to awaken in one's own soul through acceptance of the impulse of the Christmas Conference. Full awakening, however, occurs only in the First Class of the School of Spiritual Science founded after the Christmas Conference, where every anthroposophist is still seriously *tested* as to whether he or she can recognize in this School the true Michael substance, and as a result is willing courageously to stand up for this substance as its Guardian and care-taker, as is proper for a true Michaelite. For only by taking into one's own heart this Michael substance, contained as it is in the mantric wealth of the First Class, does Michael himself begin to live in it. Then, the following words by Rudolf Steiner will gradually become a fully valid reality: 'Michael, who has striven down from the Sun for the sake of those who behold the spiritual in the cosmos, Michael intends in the future to take up his abode in the hearts, in the souls, of human beings on Earth' (GA 240, 21 August 1924).

These are the deeper reasons — and more could be added — that are of decisive significance for our decision to become members of the School of Spiritual Science; reasons that can guide us to this Michael School that rightfully exists on Earth. Let us sum up these reasons once more at the end of these expositions. First, it is a matter of hearing the voice of the Guardian who speaks today on behalf of Michael to anthroposophists, and the voluntary decision to follow his call. Next, courage is asked for and whether one is willing uncompromisingly to profess to this voice so as then to begin with the awakening at the Threshold of the spiritual world. This path then leads us further into the Michael School on Earth where we are tested regarding our karmic relationship to Michael through our own dealing with the Michaelic substance of its mantric contents.

*

In conclusion, one further motif must not remain unmentioned. For the School of Spiritual Science consists from the beginning not merely of the First Class, meaning the General Anthroposophical Section, but also the various specialized Sections.[43] What is intended with these sections? If the First Class leads us through its course of 19 stages in an ever more all-encompassing experience of the Threshold to the spiritual world — meaning to reach the Threshold and consciously to cross it — then the opposite movement, that closes each Class lesson, is of equal importance. After one has crossed the Threshold and has returned again to the earthly world, enriched by what has been experienced on yonder side of the Threshold, one is called upon to become active, creative and proficient on Earth in all domains of life through the impulses that stem from beyond the Threshold.

Since mankind already lives beyond the Threshold today, the transformation of the entirety of contemporary civilization in the sense of such a conscious crossing of the Threshold is of the greatest necessity and importance. That is why this fact has to be taken into account in the Michael School as well. In the last lecture at the Christmas Conference, Rudolf Steiner sums up this goal — which belongs among the most significant aims of the Michael School on Earth — as follows. First he reflects once more on the Christmas Conference and emphasizes that it is capable of bestowing an impulse on human souls that is so powerful that its effects can continue working even into the next incarnation of those human beings who have received this impulse into themselves. And this is of decisive significance for the whole further evolution of Earth civilization. 'If we can face up to this [the Guardian's stance of turning away innumerable human souls at the Threshold of the spiritual world] in our soul in all earnestness during this conference, then *this Christmas Conference* will send a strong impulse into our souls. That impulse can then carry our souls away to do strong work of the kind needed by humanity today, so that in their next incarnation human beings will be able to encounter the

Guardian of the Threshold properly, or rather in order that *civilization as a whole will measure up to the Guardian of the Threshold'* (GA 260, 1 January 1924).

In this, the most important task of the various Sections of the School of Spiritual Science at the Goetheanum is expressed. First, the General Anthroposophical Section has to bring individual human beings far enough along the path of inner schooling so that in full wakefulness and composure they are able to reach and cross over the Threshold to the spiritual world. For only from yonder side of the Threshold come the spiritual forces that can actually transform earthly civilization. After that, through the special Sections becoming functional, our civilization must be so renewed and changed by the above-mentioned spiritual forces so that in the future (though perhaps not until their second or third incarnation after our age) human beings — trained in the right way by this Michael School — will bring earthly civilization so far that it can measure up to the stern testing of the Guardian of the Threshold. Only thereby will humanity even begin to attain its actual goal on Earth. What this signifies can only be answered with the words by Rudolf Steiner: 'It is a matter of utmost enormous importance!' (GA 240, 19 July 1924.)

Currently in the School of Spiritual Science and its Sections, one can only begin with the very first steps in the above direction. Yet we must clearly be aware that if civilization does not enter upon this path in freedom then, due to the already mentioned reasons, civilization will move towards ever-increasing decline and ultimate dis-integration. In the concluding lecture of the Christmas Conference, Rudolf Steiner speaks in this regard of the danger that otherwise Earth will become completely 'barbarized' (ibid.). From this perspective, one can recognize the deep seriousness and great responsibility one is charged with today. It is the responsibility, while fully acknowledging each single person's individual freedom, which cannot be separated from the reply to the question: Why do I become a member of the First Class of the Michael School?

Appendix: *The Philosophy of Freedom* and the Supersensible Preparation of Anthroposophy

From the contents of *The Philosophy of Freedom* primarily, we can gather the actual form in which the two above-described stages of anthroposophy's supersensible preparation have found their human replica in this book. In his last appendix to the new edition of 1918, Rudolf Steiner mentions that it is the 'philosophical foundation' for all his 'later writings' (GA 4), meaning for the whole of anthroposophy, that he once designated as 'the gift by Michael' (GA 152, 2 May 1913). This is why it is implied (in the subject itself) that in *The Philosophy of Freedom* one finds the two fundamental characteristics of the mighty Michael Mystery, in regard to the earthly human being, as if in a 'philosophical reflection'.

The first characteristic consists in the fact that, following the Mystery of Golgotha, the cosmic intelligence (which had previously been administered by Michael from out of the Sun) descended to the Earth where it became human intelligence. Now, in this regard our task consists of spiritualizing this intelligence in our soul in such a way that Michael can take it back, so that a completely new relationship will originate between him and humanity. A group of human souls was prepared for this task in the Michael School. The path to its realization on Earth is described in the first part of *The Philosophy of Freedom*, where the attainment of 'intuitively experienced thinking' is outlined; whereby 'the human being is also transposed into a spiritual world as one who cognizes' and with that can enter into a new, completely free, relationship to Michael.

The second part of *The Philosophy of Freedom* deals with the free deeds by human beings — grasped in body-free thinking out of moral intuitions — that are taken up by Michael into his cosmic domain where 'what is a human deed on Earth' becomes 'cosmic deed' (GA 233a, 13 January 1924). And the inner faculty to carry out such actions was especially cultivated in human souls in the Cosmic Michael Cultus (the second stage of the supersensible preparation of the Michael School). One can say that there this above-mentioned ability was actually exercised and, along with the free creating of cosmic imaginations, developed into the later seeds of 'moral imaginations' in the human being.[44]

The linkage of both parts of *The Philosophy of Freedom* takes place in its third part where 'Ultimate Questions', that is 'The Consequences of Monism', are dealt with, subjects that are pursued in this book as its main orientation. There it is shown how a person can fully consciously fit his or her 'individual existence into the life of the cosmos' so as to encounter Michael there, and at the same time ascend into a true 'life in God' while still on Earth; a condition that, since the Mystery of Golgotha, signifies the life and working together with Christ.

With this the modern path to Michael–Christ is already traced out, which in the final part of the *Philosophy of Freedom* is summed up in compressed form as the epistemological basis for what Rudolf Steiner at the end of his life would be presenting, based on his spirit-research as the Michael–Christ Mystery on Earth and in the cosmos.[45]

Furthermore, in this book we deal with 'results of *introspective* observation following the *methods of natural science*' — something that is a direct result of the first event (the powerful super-sensible tempest) through which human beings experienced such a transformation that they became 'head beings'. It was based on this event that the development of natural science and its method became possible for humanity in the first place.

Notes

1. GA 118.
2. This is why Rudolf Steiner does not link the genuine 'Masters of Wisdom and Harmony of Feeling' with Eastern wisdom but principally with a deeper comprehension of the Christ Being and the Mystery of Golgotha. He says in this regard: 'Those who have understood that the progress of humanity depends on the comprehension of the mighty event of Golgotha are those who as the Masters of Wisdom and Harmony of Feeling are united in the great leading lodge of humanity' (GA 107, 22 March 1909). This lodge was guided on Atlantis by the leading Christ- initiate of the Sun Oracle. In theosophical literature he was called Manu. Concerning the Rosicrucian masters, see above all the lecture of 31 August 1909 (GA 113).
3. Concerning the expression, 'spiritual powers in regard to the Michael being', Rudolf Steiner writes: 'The *spiritual powers* that are designated by the name, Michael, administer the ideas in the spiritual cosmos' (article: 'The Human Soul Condition before the Dawn of the Michael Epoch', GA 26). We see here the mediating beings who work between Michael and humanity. On this see also S. O. Prokofieff, *Relating to Rudolf Steiner*, Part II, Chap. 4, 'Working with the New Group Souls', Temple Lodge 2008.
4. See in more detail in S. O. Prokofieff, *Rudolf Steiner und die Meister des Esoterischen Christentums* ('Rudolf Steiner and the Masters of Esoteric Christendom'), in press.
5. As he did in the opening address of the Christmas Conference, in regard to the beginning of the contemporary Michael epoch, Rudolf Steiner speaks in many other passages of the 'last third of the nineteenth century,' which

began, precisely dated, in 1867. Thus the establishment of the Theosophical Society already falls within this time period. What was just stated does not, however, contradict the fact that in the narrower sense the Michael epoch did not start until 1879, for this date applies above all to the whole of humanity. 'The last third', on the other hand, indicates the span of time when at the outset only the initiates could hear Michael's call.

6. See on this also S.O. Prokofieff: *The Foundation Stone Meditation, A Key to the Christian Mysteries,* Chap. 6, 'The Merging of the Rosicrucian and the Michaelic Stream in the Foundation Stone Meditation', Temple Lodge 2006.

7. See also the essay, 'Fortsetzung der zweiten Betrachtung: Hemmungen und Förderungen der Michael-Kräfte im aufkommenden Zeitalter der Bewußtseinsseele ('Continuation of the second consideration: Obstacles and facilitations regarding the Michael forces in the coming age of the consciousness soul', GA 26). More details concerning the correlation of the Rosicrucian and the Michaelic stream can be found in Chap. 6.

8. See S. O. Prokofieff, *Anthroposophy and The Philosophy of Freedom,* Chap. 11, 'The Rosicrucian and Michaelic Impulse in *The Philosophy of Freedom*', Temple Lodge 2008.

9. In the lectures following the Christmas Conference, and even in the Class Lessons, Rudolf Steiner speaks at the outset only about the 'renewal of the Mysteries'. However, at the end of the public lecture that he gave on 26 May 1924 in Paris under the title 'How to Gain Knowledge of the Supersensible World', he refers quite unexpectedly to the New Mysteries several times. There it says: 'Quietly and not as loudly as in the old Mysteries, the students of spiritual wisdom will approach the new Mysteries, Mysteries that once again bring human beings the message of the eternal in man and the world that is so necessary' (GA 84). And then he adds: 'What thirsts in a few

human beings consciously for the spiritual world can only be satisfied through the modern Mysteries. One who deals honestly with the spiritual world looks for a will in human beings that will quite certainly be born; a will for the *new Mysteries*, for spirituality will only arise among human beings, when *new* Mysteries originate where human beings will find the spirit in a more pondering, light-filled manner than they did in the old Mysteries' (ibid.). Then, at the end of his teaching activity, shortly before the final days on his sick-bed, he spoke in September 1924 of the *new Mysteries* for the first time. Thus, on the occasion of the lecture cycle *The Book of Revelation* for the priests of the Christian Community, he told them: 'We have designated what can make the Christian Community the bearer of an essential part of the new Mysteries' (GA 346, 7 September 1924). Earlier too, at the beginning of the cycle, he had spoken of the 'new age of the Mysteries' (elsewhere, 5 September 1924) in regard to the fourth epoch of the Mystery-development of humanity in which the new Mysteries must replace the previous 'half-new' ones. One can well imagine that it was only due to illness that Rudolf Steiner was not permitted to elaborate on and speak more precisely about the secrets of the new Christian Mysteries, whose founding had been carried out at the Christmas Conference of 1923/1924 (See more on this in S. O. Prokofieff, *May Human Beings Hear It!*, Temple Lodge 2004).

10. Edwin Froböse, Friedrich Hiebel and Karl von Baltz were the ones I spoke to about this at that time.

11. That Michael is referred to in a hidden form when, during the Christmas Conference, reference is made again and again to the 'signs of the present' or 'signs of the time' (GA 260, 25 December 1923), is something that has been mentioned elsewhere. See *May Human Beings Hear It!*, Chap. 2, 'The Mystery Act of the Foundation Stone Laying on 25 December 1923', Temple Lodge 2004.

12. See more in S. O. Prokofieff, *The Esoteric Significance of Spiritual Work in Anthroposophical Groups*, Temple Lodge 2007.

13. Only the Rosicrucians knew something about this lofty secret of humanity's evolution. Rudolf Steiner points to this in the words that follow directly after a description of the cosmic tempest: 'It was in the first third of the fifteenth century; it was during the time when behind the scenes of modern development the Rosicrucian School was founded.' (ibid.)

14. One can also note that these three events correspond to ego-development as described in the Foundation Stone Meditation.

15. In human life, such a comprehension of anthroposophy signifies a gift, brought along into Earth-incarnation, of being able to utilize one's healthy human reason independently of one's corporeality.

16. In the essay, 'Where is the Human Entity As a Thinking and Memory-Possessing Being?' (GA 26), Rudolf Steiner writes about the fact that Michael's world in the cosmos is the 'world of rhythm'.

17. These three stages of the heavenly preparation of anthroposophy correspond to the threefold configuration of the hierarchical cosmos. In the first stage, the creative impulse comes out of the domain of the First Hierarchy; the Michael School unfolds its instructional activity in the Sun Sphere, which is the primal homeland of the Second Hierarchy; ultimately the supersensible cultus takes place in the Moon domain, from which the Third Hierarchy is primarily active.

18. Rudolf Steiner also speaks of this 'new spirit' of the Christmas Conference in the Class Lessons.

19. Likewise the karma reflections that followed after the Christmas Conference were given by Rudolf Steiner out of the same spirit of the New Mysteries. This is why he held the first lecture on karma on the day after the first Class Lesson. (See GA 235, 16 February 1924.)

20. See on this in GA 260a, 7 June 1924, and also in this chapter.

21. Here and in other passages during the Christmas Conference, the words 'signs of the time' refer in veiled form to the Michael Impulse. (See more on this in *May Human Beings Hear It!*, Chap. 2, 'The Mystery Act of the Foundation Stone Laying on 25 December 1923', Temple Lodge 2004.)

22. The fact that Rudolf Steiner intended to write a second part for this book, something he was prevented from doing, possibly points in the same direction.

23. See more in Note 34.

24. See about the relationship between the Threshold and the Guardian to the knowledge of evil in S. O. Prokofieff: *The Guardian of the Threshold and The Philosophy of Freedom*, Chap. 6 'The Secret of Evil and the Greater Guardian of the Threshold', Temple Lodge 2011.

25. See Margarete and Erich Kirchner-Bockholt, *Rudolf Steiner's Mission and Ita Wegman*, Rudolf Steiner Press, London 1977.

26. In his Christmas lectures of 1920, Rudolf Steiner speaks of the inner metamorphosis of the Kings and Shepherds after the Turning Point of Time. If both groups were actually to take to heart the impulse of the Mystery of Golgotha, then the Kings should have developed the characteristics of the Shepherds in themselves, and the Shepherds those of the Kings. This means: the Kings who previously sought the spiritual wisdom (Sophia) in the widths of the cosmos must now find this wisdom as 'inner astronomy', in themselves, as evolution of worlds in the sense of *Occult Science, an Outline*. And the Shepherds, who sought the spiritual wisdom (Sophia) in their hearts, must now find it based on the spiritualized experience of the external world in all of nature. In so doing, the former (the Kings) worked more out of the impulse of knowledge [*Erkenntnis*], the latter (the Shepherds) more out of the will. (See GA 202, 23 and 25 December 1920.) So one can say: The first Goetheanum was constructed out of

the Christianized cognition (or Knowledge) of the Kings, whilst the model of the second building was created by Rudolf Steiner out of the Christianized will of the Shepherds.

27. See Ita Wegman: *An die Freunde* (To the friends), article: 'Das alte und das neue Goetheanum' (The Old and the New Goetheanum), 3 May 1925, Arlesheim 1968.

28. Within the Third Hierarchy, the Archai have, as their outer sheath, what lives as the fourth member of the 'I' in the human being. Correspondingly, the astral body represents the outer garment of the Archangeloi. Angels bear as their outer sheath the ether body; human beings, the physical body.

29. That the path into the spiritual world, as depicted in both books, has retained its full significance, even following the founding of the First Class, is affirmed by the reference to both in the fourteenth Class Lesson.

30. See GA 158, 11 April 1912.

31. See about the subterranean ahrimanic rival school in GA 240, 20 July 1924.

32. Before this unlearning of thinking reaches the level of everyday thinking, it shows its symptoms in a more subtle way, inasmuch as the human being first loses the ability to think *spiritual* thoughts. A striking symptom in this direction is that nowadays one even hears from anthroposophists: We no longer understand Rudolf Steiner's speech — it is difficult, unusual, outdated, and so on. In reality, the problem is not Rudolf Steiner's language at all — which is unusual only in the sense that he has elevated the German language to the Mystery language of the Fifth Post-Atlantean Cultural Epoch — the problem is with the readers themselves, who by means of this symptom should in fact notice that in reality they can no longer think the spiritual thoughts that are brought to expression through Rudolf Steiner's speech.

33. See in S. O. Prokofieff: *The East in the Light of the West, Parts 1–3*, Temple Lodge 2010.

34. This process is in reality connected with the nature of the Eighth Sphere, the origin of which has to be traced back to how the luciferic spirits bring imaginations of the Ancient Moon in an inappropriate manner to Earth evolution, where these imaginations are then pervaded with earthly matter by ahrimanic spirits. In this way, these purely spiritual imaginations assume a terrestrially visible character, and as a result thus attain a resemblance to the physical world of senses. (See GA 254, 18 October 1915.)

35. Ahriman, too, will try during his incarnation at the beginning of our millennium to combine clairvoyance with materialism, and to achieve this, he will launch a 'great mystery school' on Earth (GA 191, 15 November 1919) where, 'in grandiose manner he will turn large numbers of human beings into clairvoyants through magic arts' (ibid.); however, without any individual efforts on their part, so that such human beings 'can continue to live materialistically ... and would not need to be concerned with any spiritual striving' (ibid.).

36. See in *May Human Beings Hear It!*, Supplement III, 'Comments by the Members of the Original Executive Council on the Christmas Conference', Temple Lodge 2004.

37. It is also significant that in both addresses by the Guardian to anthroposophists, the word *courage* plays a special role. With this, the most important Michaelic virtue is pointed out, that Rudolf Steiner characterizes in the following words: 'Michael is a powerful spirit and he can only make use of courage-filled human beings; inwardly, completely courageous human beings' (GA 237, 3 August 1924).

38. See *May Human Beings Hear It!*, Chap. 2, 'The Mystery Act of the Foundation Stone Laying on 25 December 1925' Temple Lodge 2004.

39. During the Foundation Stone laying on 25 December 1923, Rudolf Steiner speaks of the necessity to grasp the spiritual realities 'with the heart as the organ of perception' (GA 260).

40. See GA 130, 5 November 1911.

41. J. E. Zeylmans van Emmichoven, *Wer war Ita Wegman?* (Who was Ita Wegman?), Vol. I, Chap., 'September 1924', Dornach, 3rd edition 2004.

42. This is why Rudolf Steiner writes at the end of the book *Knowledge of the Higher Worlds* (GA 10) that the 'white occultists ... place selfless devotion and willingness for sacrifice above all other abilities'.

43. Johannes Kühl, Bodo von Plato, Heinz Zimmermann, *The School of Spiritual Science, An Orientation and Introduction*, Temple Lodge 2010.

44. Moral imagination as a primal human faculty can naturally be developed by the human being only on Earth. The presupposition for this lies, however, in the Michael School and the imaginative cultus of the supersensible world.

45. See article in GA 26, Das Michael-Christus-Erlebnis des Menschen' (The Michael-Christ experience of the human being). Rudolf Steiner begins this article with the reference to his *Philosophy of Freedom*.

Bibliography

English titles of works by Rudolf Steiner are given only in cases where a similar (though not always identical) volume to the original German edition from the collected works — the *Gesamtausgabe* (abbreviated as 'GA') — has been published in English translation. In many cases lectures are available in typescript or in print as single lectures or compilations from the collected works. For information on these, contact Rudolf Steiner House Library, 35 Park Road, London NW1 6XT, or similar anthroposophical libraries around the world.

GA 4	*The Philosophy of Freedom* or *Intuitive Thinking as a Spiritual Path*
GA 10	*Knowledge of the Higher Worlds* or *How to Know Higher Worlds*
GA 13	*Occult Science* or *An Outline of Esoteric Science*
GA 15	*The Spiritual Guidance of the Individual and Humanity*
GA 26	*Anthroposophical Leading Thoughts*
GA 28	*The Course of My Life* or *Autobiography*
GA 109/111	*The Principal of Spiritual Economy*
GA 152	*Approaching the Mystery of Golgotha*
GA 159/160	*Das Geheimnis des Todes*
GA 233	*World History in the Light of Anthroposophy*
GA 233a	*Rosicrucianism and Modern Initiation* and *The Easter Festival*
GA 236	*Karmic Relationships — Vol. II*
GA 237	*Karmic Relationships — Vol. III*
GA 240	*Karmic Relationships — Vol. VI and VIII*
GA 260	*The Christmas Conference for the Founding of the General Anthroposophical Society 1923-1924*
GA 260a	*Die Konstitution der Allgemeinen Anthroposophischen*

	Gesellschaft und der Freien Hochschule für Geistes-wissenschaft
GA 262	*Correspondence and Documents 1901–1925*
GA 264	*From the History and Contents of the First Section of the Esoteric School 1904–1914*

All titles available via Rudolf Steiner Press (UK)
www.rudolfsteinerpress.com or SteinerBooks (USA)
www.steinerbooks.org